90 DAY SOCIAL MEDIA MARKETING

planner & workbook

BY JULIE HALL

THE SCHOOL OF MARKETING

www.juliehallonline.com. // www.theschoolofmarketing.co.uk

Hey there Marketer

Thank you for purchasing The School of Marketing Social Media Planner.

I'm Julie Hall and you can find me at The School of Marketing (www.theschoolofmarketing.co.uk) and Julie Hall Online (www.juliehallonline.com).

I'm a digital marketing and social media marketing trainer and create and sell Canva templates for coaches, experts and sole traders.

The pages inside this workbook and planner are designed to help you to get clear on how you show up on social media, think about your branding and plan out your social media content over a 90 day period. There is a lot to work through, so I occasionally run a free live workshop for my book customers to help you work through the questions on the session. Details on how to join this and upcoming dates can be found on the last page of the book. There you will also find a link to download the additional resources that are mentioned in the workbook.

This book is deliberately light on text and big on giving you the thinking space to make decisions around your social media presence and activity.

If you find it useful, I would really appreciate it if you could leave a review on your local Amazon store.

Thanks again for purchasing this book and I hope you find it useful and it supports you with your social media activity.

Happy marketing!

Julie

TABLE OF CONTENTS

TABLE OF CONTENTS

2023

JANUARY

S	M	T	W	T	F	S
1	2	3	4	5	6	7
8	9	10	11	12	13	14
15	16	17	18	19	20	21
22	23	24	25	26	27	28
29	30	31				

FEBRUARY

S	M	T	W	T	F	S
			1	2	3	4
5	6	7	8	9	10	11
12	13	14	15	16	17	18
19	20	21	22	23	24	25
26	27	28				

MARCH

S	M	T	W	T	F	S
			1	2	3	4
5	6	7	8	9	10	11
12	13	14	15	16	17	18
19	20	21	22	23	24	25
26	27	28	29	30	31	

APRIL

S	M	T	W	T	F	S
						1
2	3	4	5	6	7	8
9	10	11	12	13	14	15
16	17	18	19	20	21	22
23	24	25	26	27	28	29
30						

MAY

S	M	T	W	T	F	S
	1	2	3	4	5	6
7	8	9	10	11	12	13
14	15	16	17	18	19	20
21	22	23	24	25	26	27
28	29	30	31			

JUNE

S	M	T	W	T	F	S
				1	2	3
4	5	6	7	8	9	10
11	12	13	14	15	16	17
18	19	20	21	22	23	24
25	26	27	28	29	30	

JULY

S	M	T	W	T	F	S
						1
2	3	4	5	6	7	8
9	10	11	12	13	14	15
16	17	18	19	20	21	22
23	24	25	26	27	28	29
30	31					

AUGUST

S	M	T	W	T	F	S
		1	2	3	4	5
6	7	8	9	10	11	12
13	14	15	16	17	18	19
20	21	22	23	24	25	26
27	28	29	30	31		

SEPTEMBER

S	M	T	W	T	F	S
					1	2
3	4	5	6	7	8	9
10	11	12	13	14	15	16
17	18	19	20	21	22	23
24	25	26	27	28	29	30

OCTOBER

S	M	T	W	T	F	S
1	2	3	4	5	6	7
8	9	10	11	12	13	14
15	16	17	18	19	20	21
22	23	24	25	26	27	28
29	30	31				

NOVEMBER

S	M	T	W	T	F	S
			1	2	3	4
5	6	7	8	9	10	11
12	13	14	15	16	17	18
19	20	21	22	23	24	25
26	27	28	29	30		

DECEMBER

S	M	T	W	T	F	S
					1	2
3	4	5	6	7	8	9
10	11	12	13	14	15	16
17	18	19	20	21	22	23
24	25	26	27	28	29	30
31						

IMPORTANT DATES 2023

JANUARY

FEBRUARY

MARCH

APRIL

MAY

JUNE

JULY

AUGUST

SEPTEMBER

OCTOBER

NOVEMBER

DECEMBER

2024

JANUARY

S	M	T	W	T	F	S
	1	2	3	4	5	6
7	8	9	10	11	12	13
14	15	16	17	18	19	20
21	22	23	24	25	26	27
28	29	30	31			

FEBRUARY

S	M	T	W	T	F	S
				1	2	3
4	5	6	7	8	9	10
11	12	13	14	15	16	17
18	19	20	21	22	23	24
25	26	27	28	29		

MARCH

S	M	T	W	T	F	S
					1	2
3	4	5	6	7	8	9
10	11	12	13	14	15	16
17	18	19	20	21	22	23
24	25	26	27	28	29	30
31						

APRIL

S	M	T	W	T	F	S
	1	2	3	4	5	6
7	8	9	10	11	12	13
14	15	16	17	18	19	20
21	22	23	24	25	26	27
28	29	30				

MAY

S	M	T	W	T	F	S
	1	2	3	4	5	6
7	8	9	10	11	12	13
14	15	16	17	18	19	20
21	22	23	24	25	26	27
28	29	30	31			

JUNE

S	M	T	W	T	F	S
						1
2	3	4	5	6	7	8
9	10	11	12	13	14	15
16	17	18	19	20	21	22
23	24	25	26	27	28	29
30						

JULY

S	M	T	W	T	F	S
	1	2	3	4	5	6
7	8	9	10	11	12	13
14	15	16	17	18	19	20
21	22	23	24	25	26	27
28	29	30	31			

AUGUST

S	M	T	W	T	F	S
				1	2	3
4	5	6	7	8	9	10
11	12	13	14	15	16	17
18	19	20	21	22	23	24
25	26	27	28	29	30	31

SEPTEMBER

S	M	T	W	T	F	S
1	2	3	4	5	6	7
8	9	10	11	12	13	14
15	16	17	18	19	20	21
22	23	24	25	26	27	28
29	30					

OCTOBER

S	M	T	W	T	F	S
		1	2	3	4	5
6	7	8	9	10	11	12
13	14	15	16	17	18	19
20	21	22	23	24	25	26
27	28	29	30	31		

NOVEMBER

S	M	T	W	T	F	S
					1	2
3	4	5	6	7	8	9
10	11	12	13	14	15	16
17	18	19	20	21	22	23
24	25	26	27	28	29	30

DECEMBER

S	M	T	W	T	F	S
1	2	3	4	5	6	7
8	9	10	11	12	13	14
15	16	17	18	19	20	21
22	23	24	25	26	27	28
29	30	31				

IMPORTANT DATES 2024

JANUARY

FEBRUARY

MARCH

APRIL

MAY

JUNE

JULY

AUGUST

SEPTEMBER

OCTOBER

NOVEMBER

DECEMBER

WHY SOCIAL MATTERS

Social Media isn't about planning a great brand ...
it's about acting as if you already have one.

WHY SOCIAL MEDIA MATTERS

95% of customers expect a business to have a social media presence and 89% of them expect to be able to engage with that business online.

It can be really easy to think that the only purpose of social media is to promote your products and services, but the problem with this thinking is that **social media only works if people are engaging and connecting with your content** - otherwise they won't even see it. So don't make the mistake of making your social media all about promotion. Think about your own behaviours - what do you like? What works in terms of promotions? What makes you want to read more?

Social Media is a relationship tool first. It is a tool to share value with your audience, a tool to connect and have conversations with your customers and it is a tool to share your brand story, brand values and give them insight into your business.

It is a great way to:

- increase connection
- build authority
- add value to your customers
- entice them with your offers
- get attention
- provide support
- increase loyalty
- AND make sales.

When you are varied and targeted with your social media activity, your audience and customers will grow.

Success comes down to one thing - consistently create content that your audience wants to consume.

SECRETS OF SUCCESS

As long as you stay true to your brand, don't be afraid to take some risks with your marketing.

There is no doubt that it can be challenging to stay on top of developing a brand presence across multiple social media channels.

My advice? Pick one or two social channels at the most. Choose a channel that you enjoy interacting and engaging on and double down on your effort on that channel. Become the expert on that channel. Once you have that mastered and have a strong following, move your energy to growing the second channel. Don't make the mistake of just being present on all channels without being clear on how you are going to use that channel to grow your audience and your business.

However, make sure that you claim your social media handle across all the channels, so that it is available when you need it.

SECRETS OF SUCCESS

Don't worry if you don't find social media easy. You are not alone. It can be overwhelming, particularly if you are not a natural marketer. Start where you are, don't worry about perfection at this point - you will get better over time.

Here are some of our secrets to social media success:

Plan: Have a plan, do the thinking first and the actions become much easier.

Focus: Know what you are trying to achieve. It will help you to make the best choices.

Clarity: Who are you targeting and what do you want them to do? What is the purpose of your social media activity.

Consistency: Success will only happen if you show up every day. Consistent action will beat moments of genius every time.

Emotional connection: Create content that makes people feel something.

Resilience: Success takes time... don't worry if something doesn't get great engagement straight away, regular content, monitor what works and practice is the key to success.

SOCIAL MEDIA AUDIT

Engage, Interact, Connect and show your customer that you really understand them and they will come back again and again.

JULIE HALL

WHICH CHANNELS ARE YOU CURRENTLY ON?

Take note of where you are today and measure your progress over time. Check in each month... have your number of followers increased? (and note - you do not need to be on all the channels!)

Date:

FACEBOOK

handle: likes:

TWITTER

handle: followers:

LINKEDIN

handle: connections:

INSTAGRAM

handle: followers:

YOUTUBE

handle: subscribers:

TIKTOK

handle: followers:

PINTEREST

handle: followers:

WHICH CHANNEL(S) ARE THE MOST IMPORTANT FOR YOUR BRAND?

Given that your time is tight, which channel(s) are you going to focus most of your energy on?

SOCIAL MEDIA IMAGE SIZES

All sizes in pixels. For social posts, I tend to use the same size for all posts of 1200 x 630 except for instagram which is square. Stories and Reels are 1080 x 1920. Correct at time of publishing.

INSTAGRAM

Profile photo size: 110 x 110

Photo size: 1080 x 1080

Photo thumbnail: 161 x 161

Stories: 1080 x 1920

Reels: 1080 x 1920

Videos: 1080 x 1080 or 1080 x 1920

FACEBOOK

Cover photos: 820 x 312

Timeline photos: 1200 x 630

Stories: 1080 x 1920

Profile photos: 180 x 180

Group photo banner: 1640 x 856 (note the top and bottom of your banner will be cut on mobile devices)

FACEBOOK ADS

Feed ads: 1080 x 1080 // 1200 x 630

Right Column ads: 1080 x 1080

Marketplace ads: 1080 x 1080

Messenger inbox: 1080 x 1080

Stories: 1080 x 1920

TWITTER

Twitter profile image: 400 x 400

Twitter cover photo: 1500 x 500

Shared image: 1200 x 675 pixels

Two side by side images: 600 x 675

LINKEDIN

Personal Profile

Profile photo: 400 x 400

Cover image: 1584 x 396

LinkedIn post: 1200 x 627

Company Page

Logo size: 400 x 400

Cover image: 1128 x 191

Blog post image: 1200 x 527

PINTEREST

Profile image: 165 x 165

Pin size: 1000 x 1500 recommended

Board image size: 222 x 150

Pinterest story: 1080 x 1920

YOUTUBE

Channel cover photo: 2560 x 1440

Channel icon: 800 x 800

Video uploads: 1280 x 760

CONTENT & GRAPHICS CHECKLIST

Engage, Interact, Connect and show your customer that you really understand them and they will come back again and again.

JULIE HALL

FOR YOUR BRANDING

A color palette that you consistently apply across your content, website and social media

2-3 brand fonts that you use regularly in your social media

A professional logo, you will want a transparent png version, SVG version for easy scaling and a light version for dark backgrounds and dark version for light backgrounds

A professional looking favicon (small icon) that displays at the top of all your website and portal pages

A style guide or brand board that you can reference for use of logo, styles of images and icons and styles of photos

FOR YOUR WEBSITE & OFFER SALES PAGES

Graphics & mockups to showcase what your offer includes

Professional headshots & personal branding photos

Icons to represent key points and sections on your page

Photos and images for your website

Brand elements to include as accents for your website

CONTENT & GRAPHICS CHECKLIST

Engage, Interact, Connect and show your customer that you really understand them and they will come back again and again.

JULIE HALL

FOR YOUR PODCAST, BLOG OR CONTENT SCHEDULE

Professionally branded podcast show cover

Featured image style for each podcast episode or blog post

Posts/stories/reels to promote new episodes & blog posts

FOR YOUR SOCIAL MEDIA

Headshot or logo (square and round version for all your profile photo and brand thumbnails

Branded cover banners for all your profiles (and groups)

Story highlight icons in your brand colors

Helpful educational posts/stories/reels that provide value

Engaging relatable posts/stories/reels that drive interaction

Promotional posts/stories/reels to showcase your offers and drive traffic to your website landing & sales pages

UPCOMING PLANS

A good plan today is better than a perfect plan tomorrow

PROVERB

MONTH

MONTH

MONTH

MONTH

MONTH

MONTH

UPCOMING PLANS

Plans are nothing, planning is everything

DWIGHT D. EISENHOWER

MONTH

MONTH

MONTH

MONTH

MONTH

MONTH

Brand is the *story*

Design is the *storytelling*

SUSAN SELLERS

BRANDING

YOUR BRAND ARCHETYPE

Your brand is what people say about you when you are not in the room

JEFF BEZOS

This quote from Jeff Bezos is probably my favourites quote about branding. What I like about it, is that it shifts our thinking about our brand from being about design and towards recognising that our brand is all about how we show up in the world and the impression and value that we create.

Your brand is about how people experience you and your business. It is everything that they think, feel, hope for and know about you.

Brand archetypes are a shortcut. They are a powerful tool that can be used to help your customers identify and understand who you are and what they can expect from you but are also what will attract them to you.

Brand Archetypes work because they help you (and your customers) to see you in a particular light, that is naturally differentiated from your competitors.

Your archetype can be either who you want to be or who you already are... but the goal is to be consistent in how you reflect that archetype in your branding, your tone and how you communicate with your customers. Use it in your tone of voice, your designs, your packaging and anything else that you are putting out into the world.

Think about brands like Apple, Nike, Harley Davidson & Innocent Drinks. These companies are all extremely clear about their brand. They are easy to identify, not just because of their logo, but also because of the vibe and energy that the brand has. It's reflected in their copy, their imaging, their social media and their content. It permeates throughout their whole presence.

Your marketing becomes so easy once you embrace your brand archetype, because it's based around who you are, your values, why and how you do what you do.

DECIDING YOUR ARCHETYPE

Look at the archetypes on the following page and decide which 2 most reflect your brand. Out of the 2 you identify, choose a Primary archetype. This will be the dominant way in which your brand shows up.

Sometimes this is enough and you can stop here, but sometimes it will feel like you need to create a bit more nuance, so identify a secondary archetype that you can use to add a bit of flavour to your archetype. This might show up as adding a bit of quirkiness if your secondary archetype is the jester or leadership if it's the Ruler or Magician.

When you choose two archetypes, the Primary archetype should reflect about 70% of what your brand stands for and a Secondary archetype about 30%.

What's your archetype mix?

YOUR BRAND ARCHETYPE

If you don't give the market the story to talk about, they'll define your brand's story for you.

DAVID BRIER

THE JESTER

Friendly, Bold, Creative, Confident, Enthusiastic, Entertainer, Original, Social, Extrovert, Fun, Playful

THE LOVER

Love, Intimacy, Warmth, Committed, Magnetic, Idealistic, Sensual, Passionate, Gratitude, Beauty

THE INNOCENT

Optimistic, Kind, Pure, A Dreamer, Happy, Humble,, Gentle, Naive innocence

THE CAREGIVER

Dependable, Generous, Peaceful, Committed, Protector, Selfless, Caring, Warm, Empathetic, Accepting

THE SAGE

Teacher, Expert, Thinker, Wise, Knowledge, Truth, Guide, Mentor, Student, Authoritative

THE RULER

Ambitious, Influential, Successful, Leader, Authoritative, Powerful, Strong, Direct, Strong, In charge

THE EXPLORER

Growth, Freedom, Individual, Adventure, Daring, Pioneer, Exciting, Wanderer, Independence

THE CREATOR

Inspiring, Creative, Authentic, Vibrant, Expressive, Visionary, Passion, Pioneer, Unique, Imaginative

THE MAGICIAN

Visionary, Innovative, Transformative, Knowledgeable, Intuitive, Innovator, Charismatic

THE REBEL

Bold, Individual, Revolutionary, Changemaker, Independent, Shocking, Disruptive, Challenging

THE HERO

Courageous, Determined, Strong, Warrior, Proud, Rescuer, Focused, Competitive, Powerful

EVERYMAN/WOMAN

Friendly, Down to Earth, Humble, Loyal, Honest, Respect, Fair, Belonging, Easy going, Relaxed, Likeable

YOUR BRAND

Your brand is the single most important investment you can make in your business.

STEVE FORBES

Building a strong brand doesn't happen by accident. There are a number of key decisions and considerations that you want to plan out. The following pages will take you through the process of defining your brand and getting clear on what you want people to think about you and your business.

KNOW YOUR GOALS

Start with your brand goals first. Sometimes we think we need to create a big brand for our business to thrive, but actually, your brand might just need better defining for your market.

How do you want your brand to be perceived? What words do you want people to use to describe your brand?

WHAT ARE YOUR BRAND GOALS?

WHAT DO YOU WANT TO BE KNOWN AS / FOR?

WHERE ARE YOU NOW AGAINST THAT GOAL?

YOUR BRAND

Internalise your brand... know it, taste it, feel it, visualise it, create it, then live it.

JULIE HALL

WHAT IS YOUR BRAND ABOUT?

In one sentence, describe your brand

WHAT ARE YOUR BRAND VALUES?

What do you stand for? What is important to your brand?

WHY DO PEOPLE LOVE YOU OR YOUR BUSINESS?

What are those parts of your business that they are most attracted to?

YOUR BRAND

WHAT IS UNIQUE ABOUT YOUR BUSINESS?

There are a couple of ways to approach this... Complete this sentence: Only I ... [insert the things that only you do] OR identify those things that you do in your business that your competitors can't imitate.

YOUR BRAND PERSONALITY

What words would you use to describe your brand personality?

INTRODUCTION STATEMENT

The purpose of your introduction statement is to clearly & concisely communicate what you do and offer in 1-2 sentences. Squeezing too much detail in can make it sound wordy, scripted and just plain awkward. You want it to feel good, strong, descriptive and for it to make you feel good when you say it.

Your messaging needs to help your ideal customer see that you are the right fit for them. How you help and serve them, should be at the heart of what you communicate in your introduction statement.

There isn't one single perfectly scripted introduction that works for all scenarios and business types. The right words depend on context of the situation you are in.

You want your message to be appealing, clear, direct, memorable and credible. You don't have to be unique, but you do need to give people a good reason to work with you!

For this reason, the introduction statements inside this cheat sheet includes both first and second person narrative options.

For example, when you're asked "what do you do" it makes sense to use I/we/my/our.

For your website headline, offer tagline, SEO descriptions, social media bios and email signature, it often makes more sense to speak directly to your audience with you/your or the.

We can definitely get tunnel vision about our business and what we want to say. Ask your team, customers and peers for their thoughts and feedback. And make sure you to tell them to be honest and specific.

What you do and offer should be so clear that someone else can introduce you. Think about how you would like to be referred to when people talk about you.

INTRODUCTION STATEMENT

Here are a couple of ways you can put together your introduction statement

Your Ingredient List

SOLUTION	What is the product/service/solution you offer? e.g. Online Coaching, Classes, Training, Support, Strategy
ADJECTIVE	What's special about it? Describe it with 1-2 words. e.g Fast & simple, professional, qualified, smart, useful
PEOPLE	What type of people need this? Describe them in 1-2 words. e.g. Single parents, artists, introverts, health coaches
BENEFIT	What's the desirable outcome, result or benefit? e.g. Save time, increase sales, more confidence, less stress
PROBLEM	What struggle, pain point or problem do you help solve? e.g. Tech overwhelm, low confidence, lack of time, anxiety
TITLE	How do you refer to yourself professionally in 2-3 words? e.g. [Niche] Coach, Expert, Mentor, Consultant, Specialist, Teacher, Creator, Artist, Entrepreneur, Leader, Advocate

YOUR TURN...

SOLUTION

ADJECTIVE

PEOPLE

BENEFIT

PROBLEM

TITLE

INTRODUCTION STATEMENT

Now you've nailed the key points your audience needs to know, swap the following prompts and experiment with the structure, tone and narrative of your introduction statement.

Remember, you may need multiple versions for various scenarios. i.e. In-person conversations vs. website. Whether you use first or second person narrative also depends if you're a personal brand or company.

I offer adjective solution for people who want benefit

I teach people how to benefit with adjective solution

We help people with problem so they can benefit

I'm a Title and offer adjective solution to help benefit

I'm a Title for people who want to improve problem or benefit

Learn how to benefit with adjective solution

Adjective solution to help problem, so you can benefit

Solution for people who want to improve problem or benefit

Benefit or solve problem with adjective solution

Title helping you benefit with adjective solution

YOUR TURN...

YOUR SOCIAL MEDIA BIO

WRITE A SHORT SOCIAL BIO TO USE ON YOUR PLATFORMS

Your bio should be interesting, engaging and give people an idea what you are about.

CREATE A SUMMARY SOCIAL BIO

Sometimes you only have a limited number of characters to use in your business biography box, so create a shorter version here.

YOUR SOCIAL MEDIA PRESENCE

DESCRIBE YOUR SOCIAL MEDIA TONE OF VOICE

What adjectives would you use to describe your social media tone of voice ? For example friendly, formal, fun, cheeky etc (you can also think in term if 'this, not that').

IF YOUR BRAND WAS A CELEBRITY...

Sometimes it's easier to think about our brand metaphorically. If you could choose a celebrity that is a brand match in terms of style, values and personality, who would it be? It can also be a combination of 2 celebrities if you can't think of just one!

WHAT ARE YOUR SOCIAL MEDIA OBJECTIVES?

Intent: Delight ... Engage... Inform ... Educate ... Inspire ... Help ... Promote ... Connect ... Excite... Entice... Feel good factor?

BRAND BOARD

LOGO

You want to have a round version, landscape version and square version of your logo that you can use across your social channels. We also recommend that you have a white / light version for use on dark backgrounds and a dark version for use on light backgrounds.

HEXIDECIMAL CODES

Keep your colour palette simple. 4-6 colour maximum recommended. Make a note of your hexadecimal colour codes (they start with #) below for easy reference when you are creating your graphics.

FONTS AND FONT FAMILIES

Which fonts will you use for your social media graphics?

BRANDING NOTES

Good marketers see customers as *complete* human beings with all the dimensions *real people* have

JONAH SACHS

KNOW YOUR CUSTOMER

KNOW YOUR CUSTOMER

The better you know your customer, the more targeted and effective your social media marketing will be. Don't make the mistake of trying to market to everyone, this will end up meaning that you are marketing to no-one.

You want your social media posts to connect and resonate with your ideal audience. This means creating captions and using images that will help your perfect customer to recognise themselves and respond.

You want to inspire them, speak to their challenges and desires, and create the right messaging that means that they take action with you.

CREATING YOUR CUSTOMER PERSONA

Each product and service you offer should have it's own Customer Persona and you might find that you have multiple avatars in your business. There may be some crossover between them, but you are likely to find that they have unique characteristics. Some products and services may have multiple avatars. I like to work on the 80/20 principle and focus on those elements that are differentiating and important (ie if gender doesn't matter, don't worry about it). It's important that you think of your persona as an individual, rather than a faceless group as it will help you to create content and posts that speak to them on a personal level.

Another shortcut is to think of someone who is an existing ideal customer. That way you have a strong starting point for building out your persona.

If you would like to go deeper on learning more about your customer, go to https://juliehallonline.com/smpresources to get downloadable customer versions of the customer persona sheets.

CUSTOMER PERSONA PROMPTS

- Who are they?
- Do they have any defining characteristics?
- What do they have in common?
- What challenges are they facing?
- What desires do they have?
- What will success look like for them?
- How does that make them feel?
- Where are they looking for answers?
- Where do they hangout online?
- What questions are they asking?
- What have they tried already?
- What isn't working for them?
- Why haven't they succeeded already?
- Are they actively looking for the solution you are offering?

KNOW YOUR CUSTOMER

There are two ways you can define your customer... you can go through an intellectual exercise where you outline the traits about your ideal customer and then hone it down to an imaginary figure that you have identified as your perfect customer or you can go and speak to some of your existing customers that are your ideal customer.

You may have got the impression that option 2 is my preferred option, and you'd be right. The reason for this is that you can have a conversation about what they love about your brand and you. You will learn what their real challenges are, not just their imagined ones and you can discover what the most important things are to them and how you can support them best.

Here are some ways you can find out more about your customer

TALK TO THEM

Know some people you think are a fit as your ideal customer? Ask them if they are up for a coffee and ask some questions to find out more about their likes, dislikes and lives.

CREATE A POLL

A great and fast way to see what your clients want is to find a Facebook group in your niche, and ask a question via a poll.

EMAIL A SURVEY

Have an email list with so clients already? Email out a survey to find out a bit more information about who you are currently serving.

ANALYTICS

Chances are you already have a social media platform, or website. Look at the analytics and demographics to find out more about your ideal customers.

COMPETITORS

Know a competitor? Go to their social media and have a look at who is currently interacting with their brand.

ELIMINATION

Sometimes the best way to learn more is to write a list of what your ideal customer is not!

As your business grows, you will get more and more clarity around who you serve.

Try to keep your research as close as you can to reality

CUSTOMER BRAINSTORM

Spend a few minutes writing down everything that you know about your customer using the prompts and the results from your customer research.

CUSTOMER BRAINSTORM

B2C CUSTOMER PERSONA

PHOTO:

NAME:

GENDER:

AGE:

LOCATION:

INCOME:

EDUCATION:

OCCUPATION:

STATUS:

_______________:

BRAND LIKES

INTERESTS

THEY VALUE

HOW THEY LIKE TO HEAR FROM YOU

INSIGHTS / STORY

NEEDS / WANTS / DESIRES

CHALLENGES / WORRIES / CONCERNS

B2B CUSTOMER PERSONA

PHOTO:

NAME:

GENDER: AGE:

LOCATION: SENIORITY

COMPANY TURNOVER & SIZE

JOB TITLE

HOW THEY BUY

WHAT MATTERS

HOW THEY LIKE TO HEAR FROM YOU

INSIGHTS / STORY

THEY VALUE

NEEDS / WANTS / DESIRES

CHALLENGES / WORRIES / CONCERNS

Content marketing is like a *first date*. If you only talk *about yourself*, there won't be a second one

DAVID BEEBE

CONTENT PLANNING

IMPORTANT DAYS

2023 SOCIAL MEDIA MONTHS

JANUARY

Dry January
Veganuary
Ginuary

FEBRUARY

LGBT History Month (UK)
Black History Month
National Cancer Prevention Month

MARCH

Women's History Month
Endometriosis Awareness Month
Multiple Sclerosis Awareness Month

APRIL

Stress Awareness Month (UK)
National Poetry Month
Celebrate Diversity Month

MAY

Mental Health Awareness Month
National Walking Month
Skin Cancer Awareness Month

JUNE

Pride Month
Men's Health Month
PTSD Awareness Month

JULY

National Baked Bean Month
National Ice Cream Month
World Watercolour Month

AUGUST

International Peace Month
Black Business Month
Family Fun Month

SEPTEMBER

World Alzheimer's Month
National Hispanic Heritage Month (US)
Back To School

OCTOBER

Black History Month (UK)
Breast Cancer Awareness Month
Domestic Violence Awareness Month

NOVEMBER

Movember (Men's Health Awareness)
NaNoWriMo
National Diabetes Month (US)

DECEMBER

AIDS Awareness Month
Holiday Season

2023 SOCIAL MEDIA DAYS

JANUARY DAYS

01: New Year's Day
02: Science Fiction Day
02: Bank Holiday
04: World Braille Day
05: National Bird Day
06: National Technology Day
08: Bubble Bath Day
09: Clean Your Desk Day
10: Houseplant Appreciation Day
14: Dress Up Your Pet Day
15: National Hat Day
15: World Religion Day
16: Blue Monday
17: Big Energy Saving Week
19: Popcorn Day
19: Get to Know Your Customers Day
21: Hugging Day
22: Chinese New Year (Year of the Rabbit)
24: Compliment Day
24: International Day of Education
25: Opposite Day
26: Australia Day
27: Holocaust Memorial Day
27: Chocolate Cake Day
28: Data Privacy Day
29: Puzzle Day
30: National Croissant Day
31: National Backward Day

FEBRUARY DAYS

02: Groundhog Day
02: World Wetlands Day
03: Golden Retriever Day
04: World Cancer Day
04: Welsh Language Music Day
04: Six Nations Rugby Begins
05: World Nutella Day
05: British Yorkshire Pudding Day
06: National Sickie Day
06: National Apprenticeship Week
06: Children's Mental Health Week
07: S Safer Internet Day
09: National Pizza Day
10: World Pulses Day
11: National Inventors' Day
11: The BRIT Awards
12: Super Bowl LVII
13: Galentine's Day
14: Valentine's Day
15: Singles Awareness Day
17: Random Acts of Kindness Day,
17: London Fashion Week (17th-20th)
19: BAFTAs
20: Love Your Pet Day
21: Shrove Tuesday (Pancake Day),
21: Mardi Gras
22: Ash Wednesday
27: National Strawberry Day, World NGO Day
28: Rare Disease Day

2023 SOCIAL MEDIA DAYS

MARCH DAYS

01: St David's Day
02: World Book Day, Dr Seuss Birthday
03: World Hearing Day
03: World Wildlife Day
04: National Grammar Day
04: National Day of Unplugging
06: National Oreo Cookie Day
06: British Pie Week (6th-12th) Begins
08: International Women's Day
10: National Pack Your Lunch Day
11: World Plumbing Day
12: Academy Awards
13: National Napping Day
14: Pi Day
15: World Consumer Rights Day
17: St. Patrick's Day
17: Red Nose Day
18: Global Recycling Day
19: Mother's Day (UK)
20: First Day of Spring,
20: International Day of Happiness
21: World Poetry Day
22: World Water Day
22: Ramadan Begins (UK)
23: National Puppy Day
25: International Waffle Day,
26: Purple Day (Epilepsy Awareness Day)
26: BST Starts
31: World Backup Day
31: Transgender Day of Visibility

APRIL DAYS

01: April Fool's Day
02: World Autism Awareness Day
03: Find a Rainbow Day
04: International Carrot Day
05: International Day of Conscience
06: US Masters Golf Begins
07: World Health Day
07: Good Friday
09: Easter Sunday
10: Easter Monday
10: Siblings Day
11: National Pet Day
12: International Day of Human Space Flight
13: Grand National 2023
14: National Gardening Day
15: World Art Day
17: Haiku Poetry Day
18: National Columnists' Day
20: National Look-Alike Day
21: National Tea Day
21: Queen Elizabeth's Birthday,
21: Ramaldan Ends
22: Earth Day, Eid al-Fitr (UK)
23: St George's Day
23: London Marathon Day
25: World Malaria Day
27: International Girls in ICT Day
28: World Day for Safety and Health at Work
29: International Dance Day
30: International Jazz Day

2023 SOCIAL MEDIA DAYS

MAY DAYS

01: May Day (Bank Holiday),

01: International Workers Day

02: World Asthma Day

03: World Press Freedom Day

04: Star Wars Day

04: International Firefighters Day,

05: Cinco de Mayo, National Space Day

06: International No Diet Day

08: World Red Cross Day

09: Europe Day

11: National Eat What You Want Day

12: International Nurses Day

12: National Limerick Day

13: World Cocktail Day

13: International Hummus Day

15: National Vegetarian Week (15th-21st)

16: International Day of Light

16: Love a Tree Day

17: World Baking Day

19: Endangered Species Day

20: World Bee Day, World Whisky Day

21: International Tea Day

21: World Meditation Day

22: World Goth Day

23: World Turtle Day

Chelsea Flower Show (23rd-27th)

25: National Wine Day

28: World Hunger Day

29: Spring Bank Holiday

30: National Creativity Day

JUNE DAYS

01: World Milk Day

01: Global Day of Parents

01: International Children's Day

01: National Fish & Chips Day

03: World Cider Day

04: International Corgi Day

05: World Environment Day

08: Best Friends Day

08: World Oceans Day

10: World Gin Day

10: UEFA Champions League Final

10: The Queen's Official Birthday

12: International Falafel Day

14: World Blood Donor Day

15: National Beer Day

15: World Tapas Day

18: Father's Day

19: National Picnic Week (19th-25th)

20: World Refugee Day

21: Summer Solstice,

21: National Selfie Day

21: World Music Day

21: International Yoga Day

22: Windrush Day

23: National Writing Day

23: Glastonbury Festival (23rd-25th)

24: Armed Forces Day

28: Eid al-Adha (28th-2nd) Begins

30: World Social Media Day

2023 SOCIAL MEDIA DAYS

JULY DAYS

01: Tour de France Begins
01: Canada Day
01: International Joke Day
02: World UFO Day
03: Wimbledon (3rd July to 16th)
04: Independence Day (US)
08: National Video Games Day
07: World Chocolate Day
07: British Grand Prix Begins
11: World Population Day
12: Simplicity Day
12: Malala Day
13: International French Fry Day
14: Bastille Day
14: National Mac and Cheese Day
15: Give Something Away Day
15: World Youth Skills Day
16: National Cherry Day
16: Ice Cream Day
17: World Day for International Justice
17: World Emoji Day
18: Nelson Mandela International Day
18: National Hot Dog Day
20: International Chess Day
24: National Tequila Day
28: World Hepatitis Day
30: International Day of Friendship
31: National Avocado Day

AUGUST DAYS

01: National Girlfriend Day
01: Respect for Parents Day
01: World Wide Web Day
04: Birmingham Commonwealth Games (4th to 11th)
04: International Beer Day
06: Cycle to Work Day
08: International Cat Day
09: Book Lovers Day
10: World Lion Day
10: International Update Your Bio Day
10: National Lazy Day
11: Son & Daughter Day
12: International Youth Day
12: World Elephant Day
13: International Left Handers Day
13: National Prosecco Day
16: National Rum Day
17: National Nonprofit Day
19: World Photography Day
19: World Humanitarian Day
19: National Potato Day
21: World Entrepreneurs Day
24: National Burger Day
25: Reading Festival (25th-27th)
26: International Dog Day
27: Notting Hill Carnival (27th-28th)
28: Summer Bank Holiday(UK)

2023 SOCIAL MEDIA DAYS

SEPTEMBER DAYS

01: National Tofu Day
02: World Coconut Day
02: International Bacon Day
02: World Beard Day
04: World Sexual Health Day
05: International Day of Charity
06: Read a Book Day
07: World Salami Day
08: International Literacy Day
10: World Suicide Prevention Day
13: Roald Dahl Day
15: Online Learning Day
16: 100 Days Until Christmas
16: Oktoberfest Begins
17: World Cleanup Day
17: World Patient Safety Day
18: International Equal Pay Day
19: Talk Like a Pirate Day
20: Pepperoni Pizza Day
21: International Day of Peace
22: World Car Free Day, Hobbit Day
23: First Day of Autumn
23: World Rivers Day
25: National Fitness Day (UK)
26: European Day of Languages
27: World Tourism Day
28: World Rabies Day
29: World Heart Day
30: International Podcast Day

OCTOBER DAYS

01: International Day of Older Persons
01: International Coffee Day
01: World Vegetarian Day
02: International Day of Nonviolence
02: World Habitat Day
03: National Techies Day
04: World Animal Day
04: National Taco Day
05: World Teacher's Day
06: National Poetry Day
06: World Smile Day
08: World Octopus Day
10: World Mental Health Day
10: World Homeless Day
11: International Day of the Girl Child
11: World Sight Day
13: World Egg Day
15: Global Handwashing Day
16: World Food Day
17: International Day for the Eradication of Poverty
19: International Gin and Tonic Day
20: International Chefs Day
21: Back to the Future Day
24: United Nations Day
25: World Pasta Day
29: Clocks Go Back (UK)
30: Checklist Day
31: Halloween, World Cities Day

2023 SOCIAL MEDIA DAYS

NOVEMBER DAYS

01: World Vegan Day
01: National Author's Day
01: National Stress Awareness Day
03: World Sandwich Day
04: National Roast Dinner Day
05: Bonfire Night
08: Cappuccino Day
08: Science, Technology, Engineering, and Medicine (STEM) Day
09: World Usability Day
11: Remembrance Day
11: Singles' Day
12: Diwali
12: Remembrance Sunday
13: World Kindness Day
14: World Diabetes Day
15: Clean Out Your Refrigerator Day
16: International Day for Tolerance
17: International Students' Day
19: International Men's Day
20: World Children's Day
21: World Hello Day
21: World Television Day
23: Thanksgiving (US)
24: Unique Talent Day, Black Friday
25: Small Business Saturday (US)
27: Cyber Monday
29: Electronic Greetings Day
30: Computer Security Day
30: St Andrew's Day

DECEMBER DAYS

01: World AIDS Day
02: English Breakfast Day
02: Small Business Saturday (UK)
03: International Day of Persons with Disabilities
04: National Sock Day
05: International Volunteer Day
05: World Soil Day
06: St Nicholas Day
06: Christmas Jumper Day
07: Hanukkah Begins
09: Christmas Card Day
10: International Animal Rights Day
10: Human Rights Day
10: Nobel Prize Day
11: International Mountain Day
14: Free Shipping Day
15: Hanukkah Ends
21: First Day of Winter
21: National Crossword Puzzle Day
24: Christmas Eve
25: Christmas Day
26: Boxing Day
27: Bank Holiday
30: No Interruptions Day
31: New Year's Eve

CONTENT IDEAS

The secret to success on social media is to create content that makes people feel something. Happy, sad, entertained, angry... make your audience take notice. Take the time to seek out and create content that is going to connect and engage them. Create content that your audience wants to read, watch, listen to. Focus on them first.

1. QUOTES

Create a document (we use google docs) and every time you see a relevant quote that you love, add it to the page so you never run out of inspiration.

2. CURATE OTHER PEOPLE'S GREAT CONTENT

At the School of Marketing we do this a lot. On Twitter we create a list of people that regularly share great content and monitor the list for content to share. You can also set up a feedly (feedly.com) account and follow other people's blogs.

3. AUDIENCE GENERATED CONTENT

Ask your customers and audience to share photos of themselves using your product or giving a testimonial or ask them for advice!

4. WATCH FOR SOMETHING IN THE NEWS THAT'S RELEVANT

Watch out for something that you can jump on in the news that is relevant to your business or service. Sometimes you can get amazing PR out of it.

5. RUN A POLL OR A SURVEY

Run a poll or a survey. Do you have a burning question? Is there something going on that you can ask an opinion about?

6. BEHIND THE SCENES CONTENT

Can you show yourself creating your products? Working with clients? Videos of your process? Your team? Your office? We all love getting an insider view.

7. SHORT VIDEO

On all social platforms video is huge and is being given priority. So create your own short videos where you share valuable nuggets of information and give your audience and customers a chance to get to know you.

8. TIPS & TUTORIALS

Your audience will never get tired of you showing them how they can use your product or service or providing information that helps them with something related to what you do! Be generous here, they will love you for it.

HASHTAGS

Hashtags are still a great way to be found by people that are interested in your products and services. Make sure you are using your hashtags in the way that the audience on your social media platform uses them.

HASHTAG GUIDELINES

Be specific
Choosing the right hashtags allows you to directly target your audience. For example, if you are selling boxing equipment, using the hashtag #sportsequipment may attract a larger audience but not all of them will be interested in boxing. By using #boxingequipment, you are talking directly to people that want what you are offering.

Not all social platforms are the same
While hashtags on all social networks have the same fundamental purpose of content tagging and discovery, the use of hashtags still varies by each social platform. As a general rule of thumb, hashtags on Instagram tend to be focused on the content of the image, whereas hashtags on Twitter are more related to a topic or subject. Hashtags are a relatively new feature on LinkedIn and shows some promise, but are rarely used on Facebook.

Instagram specifically recommends using 3-5 hashtags even though you can use up to 30, however, I recommend looking at the leaders in your field and see how many hashtags they are using.

Do your hashtag homework
Research the most popular and most relevant hashtags on a specific subject for each network. Remember, you are looking for actual customer engagement here, so choose wisely.

I recommend making a selection of a few different levels of hashtag. Ideally, you want some hashtags that have enough followers that you stay near the top of the list for a while as well as some hashtags that have a larger number of posts. I have found the sweet spot to be hashtags that have between 30,000 - 1m previous posts.

Follow **www.instagram.com/creators** to keep up to date with the lastest Instagram hashtag advice.

HASHTAGS

I like to group hasthags by content categories as this makes them easier to use and you can mix and match them to suit your post. Write your topic in the box and then identify all the other hashtags you can use with that topic.

HASHTAG TOPIC: ____________________

HASHTAG TOPIC: ____________________

HASHTAG TOPIC: ____________________

HASHTAGS

Best hashtags for use with #quotes are: #quotes #motivation #quoteoftheday #inspiration #motivationalquotes #instagood #quote #inspirationalquotes #positivevibes #lovequotes #quotestagram #quotestoliveby #wordstoliveby #lifequotes #motivation #truth #poetry

HASHTAG TOPIC: ______________________________

HASHTAG TOPIC: ______________________________

HASHTAG TOPIC: ______________________________

30 SOCIAL MEDIA PROMPTS

One of the biggest challenges is what kind of content should you start with?
Here are a few prompts to get you started

1. Tell a story about your product
2. Create a How to post for something simple related to your product / service
3. Feature a customer you have helped
4. Talk about a problem your customer has
5. Answer a frequent question you are asked
6. Create a simple checklist for something that will help your customer
7. Talk about a myth or something that lots of people get wrong in your industry
8. Talk about something that is relevant that has popped up in the news
9. Run a poll or survey
10. Ask your audience for their thoughts on something
11. Ask a fun question that is completely irrelevant to your business
12. Share a piece of your story
13. Share an insight that you have had
14. Create an inspirational quote, question or statement
15. Share a summary of a blog post / podcast / video
16. Where I / the business was last year / 2 years ago etc
17. Share a particularly useful nugget from someone else
18. Create and share a spotify playlist
19. Share a nugget from a in answer to a problem you have seen on a facebook group
20. Break a long blog post into a series of social media posts
21. Share something interesting you heard an event
22. Break a longer video into shorter social friendly videos
23. Choose a monthly theme
24. Repost previously a popular post / video
25. Share a link to your lead magnet / free download
26. Interview someone and share their insights
27. Share your most successful thing from that week
28. Share something that surprised you this week
29. Something that is new in your sector / industry / business
30. A promotion or reminder about a product that you are selling

YOUR OWN PROMPTS

CONTENT TYPES

Great content is the best sales tool in the world
MARCUS SHERIDAN

WORD

- Articles
- Blog posts
- Case studies
- Cheat sheets
- Checklists
- News & Updates
- Customer testimonials
- Ebooks
- FAQ's
- Guides
- How to's
- Interviews
- Listicles
- Product sheets
- Q&A's
- Reports
- Reviews
- Tweet stories
- White papers

IMAGE

- Art
- Candid photos
- Charts & graphs
- Collages
- Carousel posts
- Cartoons
- Illustrations
- Infographics
- Maps
- Memes
- Photos
- Mind Maps
- Processes
- Quotes
- Screenshots
- Sketched Notes
- Stock photos
- Tutorials
- Timelines

CONTENT TYPES

Stop interrupting what people are interested in and be what people are interested in

CRAIG DAVIS

DYNAMIC

- Animations
- Audiobooks
- Behind the Scenes videos
- Digital Magazines
- Live training
- Live video
- Location tours
- Podcasts
- Presentations
- Recorded events
- Slideshows
- Storyboards
- Video demonstrations
- Video case studies
- Video Interviews
- Video testimonials
- Video Walkthroughs
- Vlogs
- Webinars

INTERACTIVE

- Apps
- Calculators
- Collaborative sessions
- Contests
- Groups
- Live streams
- Live Q&A
- Photo slides
- Polls
- Quizzes
- Seminars
- Surveys
- Templates
- User generated content
- Webinars
- Worksheets
- Workshops
- Virtual working
- Word cloud

CONTENT BUCKETS

In each box below, write down a general post subject that you can write multiple social media posts for. Then in each box, write down 5 ideas for each subject and all of a sudden you have 30 ideas! Subjects can include how to's, behind the scenes, quotes, customer testimonials and more.

CONTENT TOPIC: ______________________________

TITLE IDEAS	HASHTAGS

CONTENT TOPIC: ______________________________

TITLE IDEAS	HASHTAGS

CONTENT TOPIC: ______________________________

TITLE IDEAS	HASHTAGS

CONTENT BUCKETS

Content is fire. Social media is gasoline

JAY BAER

CONTENT TOPIC: ______________________

TITLE IDEAS

HASHTAGS

CONTENT TOPIC: ______________________

TITLE IDEAS

HASHTAGS

CONTENT TOPIC: ______________________

TITLE IDEAS

HASHTAGS

IDEAS BANK

No matter what people tell you, words and ideas can change the world.

ROBYN WILLIAMS

These next two pages are a catch all for things that don't fit in the bucket OR if you are just overflowing with ideas. Try to think of ideas that really support you, your customers and your business goals. Don't be afraid to be creative. My top tip is to get a small notebook that you carry around with you or use an app on your phone that you can add new ideas to when inspiration strikes.

IDEAS BANK

The best way to have a good idea, is to have lots of ideas

LINUS PAULING

GOALS & OBJECTIVES

Start where you are. Use what you have. Do what you can.
ARTHUR ASHE

WHAT ARE YOUR SOCIAL MEDIA GOALS?

What do you want to achieve this quarter, half year, year? Try to be specific.

3 MONTH GOALS

6 MONTH GOALS

12 MONTH GOALS

UPCOMING PROMOTIONS

Think like a marketer, not a publisher
DAVID MEERMAN SCOTT

PROMOTION PLAN FOR THE NEXT 6 MONTHS

What are your promotion plans for the next 6 months? This can be campaigns or just sales plans or seasonal ideas about what you are going to be selling and promoting each month.

MONTH 1:

MONTH 2:

MONTH 3:

MONTH 4:

MONTH 5:

MONTH 6:

An hour of *planning*
can save you
10 hours of *doing*

DALE CARNEGIE

WEEKS 1-4

DATES

MONTHLY GOALS

If you set goals and go after them with all the determination you can muster, your gifts will take you places that will amaze you.

LES BROWN

GOAL 1

Goal:

Focus:

GOAL 2

Goal:

Focus:

GOAL 3

Goal:

Focus:

MONTHLY ACTION TRACKER

Consistent action is the secret to success. Write down what habits you would like to track on a regular basis such as commenting, posting regularing or creating content.

Goal

____

____

Action

____

____

M	T	W	T	F	S	S

Goal

____

____

Action

____

____

M	T	W	T	F	S	S

Goal

____

____

Action

____

____

M	T	W	T	F	S	S

THIS MONTH'S IDEAS

No matter what people tell you, words and ideas can change the world.

ROBYN WILLIAMS

TO DO LIST

The secret to success is good planning, hard work, determination and taking action

JULIE HALL

WEEKLY PLANNER

MON

TUE

WED

THU

FRI

SAT

SUN

DATES

#1 GOAL FOR THIS WEEK

ACTIONS

NOTES FOR NEXT WEEK

WEEKLY PLANNER

PRIORITIES:

	M	T	W	T	F	S	S
INSTAGRAM							
FACEBOOK							
YOUTUBE							
PINTEREST							
TIKTOK							
LINKEDIN							
TWITTER							

IDEAS & INSPIRATION:

POST PLANNING

DATE

POST / VIDEO / STORY IDEA

SUBMITTED TO:

Facebook
Pinterest
Instagram
TikTok
Twitter
YouTube
LinkedIn
Email

Likes
Comments
Link clicks / plays

DATE

POST / VIDEO / STORY IDEA

SUBMITTED TO:

Facebook
Pinterest
Instagram
TikTok
Twitter
YouTube
LinkedIn
Email

Likes
Comments
Link clicks / plays

DATE

POST / VIDEO / STORY IDEA

SUBMITTED TO:

Facebook
Pinterest
Instagram
TikTok
Twitter
YouTube
LinkedIn
Email

Likes
Comments
Link clicks / plays

POST PLANNING

DATE

POST / VIDEO / STORY IDEA

SUBMITTED TO:

Facebook
Pinterest
Instagram
TikTok
Twitter
YouTube
LinkedIn
Email

Likes
Comments
Link clicks / plays

DATE

POST / VIDEO / STORY IDEA

SUBMITTED TO:

Facebook
Pinterest
Instagram
TikTok
Twitter
YouTube
LinkedIn
Email

Likes
Comments
Link clicks / plays

DATE

POST / VIDEO / STORY IDEA

SUBMITTED TO:

Facebook
Pinterest
Instagram
TikTok
Twitter
YouTube
LinkedIn
Email

Likes
Comments
Link clicks / plays

NOTES

NOTES

WEEKLY PLANNER

MON

TUE

WED

THU

FRI

SAT

SUN

DATES

#1 GOAL FOR THIS WEEK

ACTIONS

NOTES FOR NEXT WEEK

WEEKLY PLANNER

PRIORITIES:

	M	T	W	T	F	S	S
INSTAGRAM							
FACEBOOK							
YOUTUBE							
PINTEREST							
TIKTOK							
LINKEDIN							
TWITTER							

IDEAS & INSPIRATION:

POST PLANNING

DATE

POST / VIDEO / STORY IDEA

SUBMITTED TO:

Facebook
Pinterest
Instagram
TikTok
Twitter
YouTube
LinkedIn
Email

Likes
Comments
Link clicks / plays

DATE

POST / VIDEO / STORY IDEA

SUBMITTED TO:

Facebook
Pinterest
Instagram
TikTok
Twitter
YouTube
LinkedIn
Email

Likes
Comments
Link clicks / plays

DATE

POST / VIDEO / STORY IDEA

SUBMITTED TO:

Facebook
Pinterest
Instagram
TikTok
Twitter
YouTube
LinkedIn
Email

Likes
Comments
Link clicks / plays

POST PLANNING

DATE

POST / VIDEO / STORY IDEA

SUBMITTED TO:

Facebook
Pinterest
Instagram
TikTok
Twitter
YouTube
LinkedIn
Email

Likes
Comments
Link clicks / plays

DATE

POST / VIDEO / STORY IDEA

SUBMITTED TO:

Facebook
Pinterest
Instagram
TikTok
Twitter
YouTube
LinkedIn
Email

Likes
Comments
Link clicks / plays

DATE

POST / VIDEO / STORY IDEA

SUBMITTED TO:

Facebook
Pinterest
Instagram
TikTok
Twitter
YouTube
LinkedIn
Email

Likes
Comments
Link clicks / plays

NOTES

NOTES

WEEKLY PLANNER

MON

TUE

WED

THU

FRI

SAT

SUN

DATES

#1 GOAL FOR THIS WEEK

ACTIONS

NOTES FOR NEXT WEEK

WEEKLY PLANNER

PRIORITIES:

	M	T	W	T	F	S	S
INSTAGRAM							
FACEBOOK							
YOUTUBE							
PINTEREST							
TIKTOK							
LINKEDIN							
TWITTER							

IDEAS & INSPIRATION:

POST PLANNING

DATE

POST / VIDEO / STORY IDEA

SUBMITTED TO:

- Facebook
- Instagram
- Twitter
- LinkedIn
- Pinterest
- TikTok
- YouTube
- Email

Likes

Comments

Link clicks / plays

DATE

POST / VIDEO / STORY IDEA

SUBMITTED TO:

- Facebook
- Instagram
- Twitter
- LinkedIn
- Pinterest
- TikTok
- YouTube
- Email

Likes

Comments

Link clicks / plays

DATE

POST / VIDEO / STORY IDEA

SUBMITTED TO:

- Facebook
- Instagram
- Twitter
- LinkedIn
- Pinterest
- TikTok
- YouTube
- Email

Likes

Comments

Link clicks / plays

POST PLANNING

DATE

POST / VIDEO / STORY IDEA

SUBMITTED TO:

Facebook
Pinterest
Instagram
TikTok
Twitter
YouTube
LinkedIn
Email

Likes
Comments
Link clicks / plays

DATE

POST / VIDEO / STORY IDEA

SUBMITTED TO:

Facebook
Pinterest
Instagram
TikTok
Twitter
YouTube
LinkedIn
Email

Likes
Comments
Link clicks / plays

DATE

POST / VIDEO / STORY IDEA

SUBMITTED TO:

Facebook
Pinterest
Instagram
TikTok
Twitter
YouTube
LinkedIn
Email

Likes
Comments
Link clicks / plays

NOTES

NOTES

WEEKLY PLANNER

MON

TUE

WED

THU

FRI

SAT

SUN

DATES

#1 GOAL FOR THIS WEEK

ACTIONS

NOTES FOR NEXT WEEK

WEEKLY PLANNER

PRIORITIES:

	M	T	W	T	F	S	S
INSTAGRAM							
FACEBOOK							
YOUTUBE							
PINTEREST							
TIKTOK							
LINKEDIN							
TWITTER							

IDEAS & INSPIRATION:

POST PLANNING

DATE

POST / VIDEO / STORY IDEA

SUBMITTED TO:

Facebook
Pinterest
Instagram
TikTok
Twitter
YouTube
LinkedIn
Email

Likes

Comments

Link clicks / plays

DATE

POST / VIDEO / STORY IDEA

SUBMITTED TO:

Facebook
Pinterest
Instagram
TikTok
Twitter
YouTube
LinkedIn
Email

Likes

Comments

Link clicks / plays

DATE

POST / VIDEO / STORY IDEA

SUBMITTED TO:

Facebook
Pinterest
Instagram
TikTok
Twitter
YouTube
LinkedIn
Email

Likes

Comments

Link clicks / plays

POST PLANNING

DATE

POST / VIDEO / STORY IDEA

SUBMITTED TO:

Facebook

Pinterest

Instagram

TikTok

Twitter

YouTube

LinkedIn

Email

Likes

Comments

Link clicks / plays

DATE

POST / VIDEO / STORY IDEA

SUBMITTED TO:

Facebook

Pinterest

Instagram

TikTok

Twitter

YouTube

LinkedIn

Email

Likes

Comments

Link clicks / plays

DATE

POST / VIDEO / STORY IDEA

SUBMITTED TO:

Facebook

Pinterest

Instagram

TikTok

Twitter

YouTube

LinkedIn

Email

Likes

Comments

Link clicks / plays

NOTES

NOTES

MONTHLY RESULTS

To be great at marketing requires you first to be brave

JULIE HALL

You get what you measure. So use this page to track your progress against the monthly goals you identified earlier. How did you do? What can you improve? What went well?

GOAL 1: ______________________

On a scale of 1-10 how did you do against that goal?

GOAL 2: ______________________

On a scale of 1-10 how did you do against that goal?

GOAL 3: ______________________

On a scale of 1-10 how did you do against that goal?

RESULTS

There are no secrets to success. It is the result of preparation, hard work, and learning from failure.

COLIN POWELL

WHAT I HAVE ACHIEVED THIS MONTH IS...

WHAT I AM MOST PROUD OF IS...

WHAT I AM GOING TO DO DIFFERENTLY NEXT MONTH IS...

WHAT'S WORKING REALLY WELL IS...

If you don't know
where you are going,
you'll end up
someplace else

YOGI BERRA

WEEKS 5-8

DATES

MONTHLY GOALS

Successful people do things that the average person is not willing to do. They make sacrifices the average person is not willing to make. But the difference it makes is extraordinary.

BRIAN TRACY

GOAL 1

Goal:

Focus:

GOAL 2

Goal:

Focus:

GOAL 3

Goal:

Focus:

MONTHLY ACTION TRACKER

Consistent action is the secret to success. Write down what habits you would like to track on a regular basis such as commenting, posting regularing or creating content.

M T W T F S S

Goal

____

____

Action

____

____

M T W T F S S

Goal

____

____

Action

____

____

M T W T F S S

Goal

____

____

Action

____

____

THIS MONTH'S IDEAS

I never made one of my discoveries through the process of rational thinking

ALBERT EINSTEIN

TO DO LIST

Always try to give extraordinary value ... your customers will love you for it

JULIE HALL

WEEKLY PLANNER

MON

TUE

WED

THU

FRI

SAT

SUN

DATES

#1 GOAL FOR THIS WEEK

ACTIONS

NOTES FOR NEXT WEEK

WEEKLY PLANNER

PRIORITIES:

	M	T	W	T	F	S	S
INSTAGRAM							
FACEBOOK							
YOUTUBE							
PINTEREST							
TIKTOK							
LINKEDIN							
TWITTER							

IDEAS & INSPIRATION:

POST PLANNING

DATE

POST / VIDEO / STORY IDEA

SUBMITTED TO:

Facebook
Pinterest
Instagram
TikTok
Twitter
YouTube
LinkedIn
Email

Likes
Comments
Link clicks / plays

DATE

POST / VIDEO / STORY IDEA

SUBMITTED TO:

Facebook
Pinterest
Instagram
TikTok
Twitter
YouTube
LinkedIn
Email

Likes
Comments
Link clicks / plays

DATE

POST / VIDEO / STORY IDEA

SUBMITTED TO:

Facebook
Pinterest
Instagram
TikTok
Twitter
YouTube
LinkedIn
Email

Likes
Comments
Link clicks / plays

POST PLANNING

DATE

POST / VIDEO / STORY IDEA

SUBMITTED TO:

Facebook
Pinterest
Instagram
TikTok
Twitter
YouTube
LinkedIn
Email

Likes
Comments
Link clicks / plays

DATE

POST / VIDEO / STORY IDEA

SUBMITTED TO:

Facebook
Pinterest
Instagram
TikTok
Twitter
YouTube
LinkedIn
Email

Likes
Comments
Link clicks / plays

DATE

POST / VIDEO / STORY IDEA

SUBMITTED TO:

Facebook
Pinterest
Instagram
TikTok
Twitter
YouTube
LinkedIn
Email

Likes
Comments
Link clicks / plays

NOTES

NOTES

WEEKLY PLANNER

MON

TUE

WED

THU

FRI

SAT

SUN

DATES

#1 GOAL FOR THIS WEEK

ACTIONS

NOTES FOR NEXT WEEK

WEEKLY PLANNER

PRIORITIES:

	M	T	W	T	F	S	S
INSTAGRAM							
FACEBOOK							
YOUTUBE							
PINTEREST							
TIKTOK							
LINKEDIN							
TWITTER							

IDEAS & INSPIRATION:

POST PLANNING

DATE

POST / VIDEO / STORY IDEA

SUBMITTED TO:

Facebook
Pinterest
Instagram
TikTok
Twitter
YouTube
LinkedIn
Email

Likes

Comments

Link clicks / plays

DATE

POST / VIDEO / STORY IDEA

SUBMITTED TO:

Facebook
Pinterest
Instagram
TikTok
Twitter
YouTube
LinkedIn
Email

Likes

Comments

Link clicks / plays

DATE

POST / VIDEO / STORY IDEA

SUBMITTED TO:

Facebook
Pinterest
Instagram
TikTok
Twitter
YouTube
LinkedIn
Email

Likes

Comments

Link clicks / plays

POST PLANNING

DATE

POST / VIDEO / STORY IDEA

SUBMITTED TO:

Facebook
Pinterest
Instagram
TikTok
Twitter
YouTube
LinkedIn
Email

Likes
Comments
Link clicks / plays

DATE

POST / VIDEO / STORY IDEA

SUBMITTED TO:

Facebook
Pinterest
Instagram
TikTok
Twitter
YouTube
LinkedIn
Email

Likes
Comments
Link clicks / plays

DATE

POST / VIDEO / STORY IDEA

SUBMITTED TO:

Facebook
Pinterest
Instagram
TikTok
Twitter
YouTube
LinkedIn
Email

Likes
Comments
Link clicks / plays

NOTES

NOTES

WEEKLY PLANNER

MON

TUE

WED

THU

FRI

SAT

SUN

DATES

#1 GOAL FOR THIS WEEK

ACTIONS

NOTES FOR NEXT WEEK

WEEKLY PLANNER

PRIORITIES:

	M	T	W	T	F	S	S
INSTAGRAM							
FACEBOOK							
YOUTUBE							
PINTEREST							
TIKTOK							
LINKEDIN							
TWITTER							

IDEAS & INSPIRATION:

POST PLANNING

DATE

POST / VIDEO / STORY IDEA

SUBMITTED TO:

Facebook
Instagram
Twitter
LinkedIn
Pinterest
TikTok
YouTube
Email

Likes

Comments

Link clicks / plays

DATE

POST / VIDEO / STORY IDEA

SUBMITTED TO:

Facebook
Instagram
Twitter
LinkedIn
Pinterest
TikTok
YouTube
Email

Likes

Comments

Link clicks / plays

DATE

POST / VIDEO / STORY IDEA

SUBMITTED TO:

Facebook
Instagram
Twitter
LinkedIn
Pinterest
TikTok
YouTube
Email

Likes

Comments

Link clicks / plays

POST PLANNING

DATE

POST / VIDEO / STORY IDEA

SUBMITTED TO:

Facebook
Pinterest
Instagram
TikTok
Twitter
YouTube
LinkedIn
Email

Likes
Comments
Link clicks / plays

DATE

POST / VIDEO / STORY IDEA

SUBMITTED TO:

Facebook
Pinterest
Instagram
TikTok
Twitter
YouTube
LinkedIn
Email

Likes
Comments
Link clicks / plays

DATE

POST / VIDEO / STORY IDEA

SUBMITTED TO:

Facebook
Pinterest
Instagram
TikTok
Twitter
YouTube
LinkedIn
Email

Likes
Comments
Link clicks / plays

NOTES

NOTES

WEEKLY PLANNER

MON

TUE

WED

THU

FRI

SAT

SUN

DATES

#1 GOAL FOR THIS WEEK

ACTIONS

NOTES FOR NEXT WEEK

WEEKLY PLANNER

PRIORITIES:

	M	T	W	T	F	S	S
INSTAGRAM							
FACEBOOK							
YOUTUBE							
PINTEREST							
TIKTOK							
LINKEDIN							
TWITTER							

IDEAS & INSPIRATION:

POST PLANNING

DATE

POST / VIDEO / STORY IDEA

SUBMITTED TO:

Facebook
Instagram
Twitter
LinkedIn
Pinterest
TikTok
YouTube
Email

Likes

Comments

Link clicks / plays

DATE

POST / VIDEO / STORY IDEA

SUBMITTED TO:

Facebook
Instagram
Twitter
LinkedIn
Pinterest
TikTok
YouTube
Email

Likes

Comments

Link clicks / plays

DATE

POST / VIDEO / STORY IDEA

SUBMITTED TO:

Facebook
Instagram
Twitter
LinkedIn
Pinterest
TikTok
YouTube
Email

Likes

Comments

Link clicks / plays

POST PLANNING

DATE

POST / VIDEO / STORY IDEA

SUBMITTED TO:

Facebook
Pinterest
Instagram
TikTok
Twitter
YouTube
LinkedIn
Email

Likes
Comments
Link clicks / plays

DATE

POST / VIDEO / STORY IDEA

SUBMITTED TO:

Facebook
Pinterest
Instagram
TikTok
Twitter
YouTube
LinkedIn
Email

Likes
Comments
Link clicks / plays

DATE

POST / VIDEO / STORY IDEA

SUBMITTED TO:

Facebook
Pinterest
Instagram
TikTok
Twitter
YouTube
LinkedIn
Email

Likes
Comments
Link clicks / plays

NOTES

NOTES

MONTHLY RESULTS

Listen to your customers, not your competitors
JOEL SPOLSKY

You get what you measure. So use this page to track your progress against the monthly goals you identified earlier. How did you do? What can you improve? What went well?

GOAL 1: ______________________________

On a scale of 1-10 how did you do against that goal?

GOAL 2: ______________________________

On a scale of 1-10 how did you do against that goal?

GOAL 3: ______________________________

On a scale of 1-10 how did you do against that goal?

MONTHLY RESULTS

Success is not final; failure is not fatal: It is the courage to continue that counts

WINSTON CHURCHILL

WHAT I HAVE ACHIEVED THIS MONTH IS...

WHAT I AM MOST PROUD OF IS...

WHAT I AM GOING TO DO DIFFERENTLY NEXT MONTH IS...

WHAT'S WORKING REALLY WELL IS...

Before anything else, *preparation* is the key to *success*

ALEXANDER GRAHAM BELL

WEEKS 9-13

DATES

MONTHLY GOALS

A dream written down with a date becomes a goal. A goal broken down into steps becomes a plan. A plan backed by action makes your dreams come true.

GREG S. REID

GOAL 1

Goal:

Focus:

GOAL 2

Goal:

Focus:

GOAL 3

Goal:

Focus:

MONTHLY ACTION TRACKER

Consistent action is the secret to success. Write down what habits you would like to track on a regular basis such as commenting, posting regularing or creating content.

M T W T F S S

Goal

____

____

Action

____

____

M T W T F S S

Goal

____

____

Action

____

____

M T W T F S S

Goal

____

____

Action

____

____

THIS MONTH'S IDEAS

Experiment with your marketing. Play. Have Fun. Your results may surprise you.

JULIE HALL

TO DO LIST

Great marketing makes your customer feel like you really understand them

JULIE HALL

WEEKLY PLANNER

MON

TUE

WED

THU

FRI

SAT

SUN

DATES

____

#1 GOAL FOR THIS WEEK

____

____

____

ACTIONS

____

____

____

____

____

____

____

____

NOTES FOR NEXT WEEK

WEEKLY PLANNER

PRIORITIES:

	M	T	W	T	F	S	S
INSTAGRAM							
FACEBOOK							
YOUTUBE							
PINTEREST							
TIKTOK							
LINKEDIN							
TWITTER							

IDEAS & INSPIRATION:

POST PLANNING

DATE

POST / VIDEO / STORY IDEA

SUBMITTED TO:

Facebook
Pinterest
Instagram
TikTok
Twitter
YouTube
LinkedIn
Email

Likes
Comments
Link clicks / plays

DATE

POST / VIDEO / STORY IDEA

SUBMITTED TO:

Facebook
Pinterest
Instagram
TikTok
Twitter
YouTube
LinkedIn
Email

Likes
Comments
Link clicks / plays

DATE

POST / VIDEO / STORY IDEA

SUBMITTED TO:

Facebook
Pinterest
Instagram
TikTok
Twitter
YouTube
LinkedIn
Email

Likes
Comments
Link clicks / plays

POST PLANNING

DATE

POST / VIDEO / STORY IDEA

SUBMITTED TO:

Facebook
Pinterest
Instagram
TikTok
Twitter
YouTube
LinkedIn
Email

Likes
Comments
Link clicks / plays

DATE

POST / VIDEO / STORY IDEA

SUBMITTED TO:

Facebook
Pinterest
Instagram
TikTok
Twitter
YouTube
LinkedIn
Email

Likes
Comments
Link clicks / plays

DATE

POST / VIDEO / STORY IDEA

SUBMITTED TO:

Facebook
Pinterest
Instagram
TikTok
Twitter
YouTube
LinkedIn
Email

Likes
Comments
Link clicks / plays

NOTES

NOTES

WEEKLY PLANNER

MON

TUE

WED

THU

FRI

SAT

SUN

DATES

#1 GOAL FOR THIS WEEK

ACTIONS

NOTES FOR NEXT WEEK

WEEKLY PLANNER

PRIORITIES:

	M	T	W	T	F	S	S
INSTAGRAM							
FACEBOOK							
YOUTUBE							
PINTEREST							
TIKTOK							
LINKEDIN							
TWITTER							

IDEAS & INSPIRATION:

POST PLANNING

DATE

POST / VIDEO / STORY IDEA

SUBMITTED TO:

Facebook
Pinterest
Instagram
TikTok
Twitter
YouTube
LinkedIn
Email

Likes
Comments
Link clicks / plays

DATE

POST / VIDEO / STORY IDEA

SUBMITTED TO:

Facebook
Pinterest
Instagram
TikTok
Twitter
YouTube
LinkedIn
Email

Likes
Comments
Link clicks / plays

DATE

POST / VIDEO / STORY IDEA

SUBMITTED TO:

Facebook
Pinterest
Instagram
TikTok
Twitter
YouTube
LinkedIn
Email

Likes
Comments
Link clicks / plays

POST PLANNING

DATE

POST / VIDEO / STORY IDEA

SUBMITTED TO:

- Facebook
- Instagram
- Twitter
- LinkedIn
- Pinterest
- TikTok
- YouTube
- Email

Likes

Comments

Link clicks / plays

DATE

POST / VIDEO / STORY IDEA

SUBMITTED TO:

- Facebook
- Instagram
- Twitter
- LinkedIn
- Pinterest
- TikTok
- YouTube
- Email

Likes

Comments

Link clicks / plays

DATE

POST / VIDEO / STORY IDEA

SUBMITTED TO:

- Facebook
- Instagram
- Twitter
- LinkedIn
- Pinterest
- TikTok
- YouTube
- Email

Likes

Comments

Link clicks / plays

NOTES

NOTES

WEEKLY PLANNER

MON

TUE

WED

THU

FRI

SAT

SUN

DATES

#1 GOAL FOR THIS WEEK

ACTIONS

NOTES FOR NEXT WEEK

WEEKLY PLANNER

PRIORITIES:

	M	T	W	T	F	S	S
INSTAGRAM							
FACEBOOK							
YOUTUBE							
PINTEREST							
TIKTOK							
LINKEDIN							
TWITTER							

IDEAS & INSPIRATION:

POST PLANNING

DATE

POST / VIDEO / STORY IDEA

SUBMITTED TO:

Facebook
Pinterest
Instagram
TikTok
Twitter
YouTube
LinkedIn
Email

Likes
Comments
Link clicks / plays

DATE

POST / VIDEO / STORY IDEA

SUBMITTED TO:

Facebook
Pinterest
Instagram
TikTok
Twitter
YouTube
LinkedIn
Email

Likes
Comments
Link clicks / plays

DATE

POST / VIDEO / STORY IDEA

SUBMITTED TO:

Facebook
Pinterest
Instagram
TikTok
Twitter
YouTube
LinkedIn
Email

Likes
Comments
Link clicks / plays

POST PLANNING

DATE

POST / VIDEO / STORY IDEA

SUBMITTED TO:

Facebook
Pinterest
Instagram
TikTok
Twitter
YouTube
LinkedIn
Email

Likes
Comments
Link clicks / plays

DATE

POST / VIDEO / STORY IDEA

SUBMITTED TO:

Facebook
Pinterest
Instagram
TikTok
Twitter
YouTube
LinkedIn
Email

Likes
Comments
Link clicks / plays

DATE

POST / VIDEO / STORY IDEA

SUBMITTED TO:

Facebook
Pinterest
Instagram
TikTok
Twitter
YouTube
LinkedIn
Email

Likes
Comments
Link clicks / plays

NOTES

NOTES

WEEKLY PLANNER

MON

TUE

WED

THU

FRI

SAT

SUN

DATES

#1 GOAL FOR THIS WEEK

ACTIONS

NOTES FOR NEXT WEEK

WEEKLY PLANNER

PRIORITIES:

	M	T	W	T	F	S	S
INSTAGRAM							
FACEBOOK							
YOUTUBE							
PINTEREST							
TIKTOK							
LINKEDIN							
TWITTER							

IDEAS & INSPIRATION:

POST PLANNING

DATE

POST / VIDEO / STORY IDEA

SUBMITTED TO:

Facebook
Pinterest
Instagram
TikTok
Twitter
YouTube
LinkedIn
Email

Likes
Comments
Link clicks / plays

DATE

POST / VIDEO / STORY IDEA

SUBMITTED TO:

Facebook
Pinterest
Instagram
TikTok
Twitter
YouTube
LinkedIn
Email

Likes
Comments
Link clicks / plays

DATE

POST / VIDEO / STORY IDEA

SUBMITTED TO:

Facebook
Pinterest
Instagram
TikTok
Twitter
YouTube
LinkedIn
Email

Likes
Comments
Link clicks / plays

POST PLANNING

DATE

POST / VIDEO / STORY IDEA

SUBMITTED TO:

Facebook
Pinterest
Instagram
TikTok
Twitter
YouTube
LinkedIn
Email

Likes
Comments
Link clicks / plays

DATE

POST / VIDEO / STORY IDEA

SUBMITTED TO:

Facebook
Pinterest
Instagram
TikTok
Twitter
YouTube
LinkedIn
Email

Likes
Comments
Link clicks / plays

DATE

POST / VIDEO / STORY IDEA

SUBMITTED TO:

Facebook
Pinterest
Instagram
TikTok
Twitter
YouTube
LinkedIn
Email

Likes
Comments
Link clicks / plays

NOTES

NOTES

WEEKLY PLANNER

MON

TUE

WED

THU

FRI

SAT

SUN

DATES

____

#1 GOAL FOR THIS WEEK

____

____

____

ACTIONS

____

____

____

____

____

____

____

____

NOTES FOR NEXT WEEK

WEEKLY PLANNER

PRIORITIES:

	M	T	W	T	F	S	S
INSTAGRAM							
FACEBOOK							
YOUTUBE							
PINTEREST							
TIKTOK							
LINKEDIN							
TWITTER							

IDEAS & INSPIRATION:

POST PLANNING

DATE

POST / VIDEO / STORY IDEA

SUBMITTED TO:

- Facebook
- Pinterest
- Instagram
- TikTok
- Twitter
- YouTube
- LinkedIn
- Email

Likes

Comments

Link clicks / plays

DATE

POST / VIDEO / STORY IDEA

SUBMITTED TO:

- Facebook
- Pinterest
- Instagram
- TikTok
- Twitter
- YouTube
- LinkedIn
- Email

Likes

Comments

Link clicks / plays

DATE

POST / VIDEO / STORY IDEA

SUBMITTED TO:

- Facebook
- Pinterest
- Instagram
- TikTok
- Twitter
- YouTube
- LinkedIn
- Email

Likes

Comments

Link clicks / plays

POST PLANNING

DATE

POST / VIDEO / STORY IDEA

SUBMITTED TO:

Facebook
Pinterest
Instagram
TikTok
Twitter
YouTube
LinkedIn
Email

Likes
Comments
Link clicks / plays

DATE

POST / VIDEO / STORY IDEA

SUBMITTED TO:

Facebook
Pinterest
Instagram
TikTok
Twitter
YouTube
LinkedIn
Email

Likes
Comments
Link clicks / plays

DATE

POST / VIDEO / STORY IDEA

SUBMITTED TO:

Facebook
Pinterest
Instagram
TikTok
Twitter
YouTube
LinkedIn
Email

Likes
Comments
Link clicks / plays

NOTES

NOTES

MONTHLY RESULTS

You have to learn the rules of the game. And then you have to play better than anyone else.
ALBERT EINSTEIN

You get what you measure. So use this page to track your progress against the monthly goals you identified earlier. How did you do? What can you improve? What went well?

GOAL 1: ______________________________

On a scale of 1-10 how did you do against that goal?

GOAL 2: ______________________________

On a scale of 1-10 how did you do against that goal?

GOAL 3: ______________________________

On a scale of 1-10 how did you do against that goal?

RESULTS

Marketing strategy will impact every piece of your business, and it should be tied to every piece of your business

BRANDON ANDERSEN

WHAT I HAVE ACHIEVED THIS MONTH IS...

WHAT I AM MOST PROUD OF IS...

WHAT I AM GOING TO DO DIFFERENTLY NEXT MONTH IS...

WHAT'S WORKING REALLY WELL IS...

Good marketing makes the *company* look smart. Great marketing makes the *customer* feel smart

JOE CHERNOV

CAMPAIGN PLANNING

CAMPAIGN PLANNING

The real fact of the matter is that nobody reads ads. People read what interests them, and sometimes it's an ad.

HOWARD LUCK GOSSAGE

WHAT ARE YOUR CAMPAIGN GOALS?

What would you like to achieve with your campaign (be as specific as possible). Choose goals that you can measure either such as clicks, conversions or sales. If you are doing a brand awareness campaign, think about how you will be able to measure the success of that campaign. One of the wonderful things about digital advertising is that we can see very quickly what is working (and what isn't). Normally you'll have one primary goals and a few secondary goals. Write yours below.

CAMPAIGN PLANNING

Creativity may well be the last legal unfair competitive advantage we can take to run over the competition

DAVE TROTT

GRAPHIC DESIGN

What kind of creative are you or your team going to create? Brainstorm some ideas here. Think about the type and style of imagery this might include. Make sure your campaign graphics fit with your brand - brand congruency is important.

ACTION PLAN

A good advertisement is one which sells the product without drawing attention to itself.

DAVID OGILVY

TASKS AND ACTIVITIES

ACTION PLAN

In our factory, we make lipstick.
In our advertising, we sell hope.
PETER NIVIO ZARLENGA

TASKS AND ACTIVITIES

CAMPAIGN PLANNING

Simplicity is the ultimate sophistication

LEONARDO DA VINCI

WHO IS YOUR AUDIENCE FOR THE CAMPAIGN

The better you know your audience, the more targeted your campaign can be.

WHAT'S YOUR BUDGET

How much are you going to invest in your campaign? Think about the total budget and daily and monthly budgets.

DO YOU NEED OTHER PEOPLE? IF SO WHO...

Do you need a graphic designer, copywriter, web person, project manager, ads specialist?

CAMPAIGN PLANNING

By definition, remarkable things get remarked upon
SETH GODIN

WHICH CHANNELS ARE YOU GOING TO FOCUS ON?

Facebook, Instagram, LinkedIn, Twitter, Pinterest, YouTube, TikTok, other?

WHAT ARE YOUR KEY MESSAGES?

What's your strapline? Key message focus? What's in it for the customer? Why are they going to want your offer? What's your call to action?

CAMPAIGN IDEAS

CAMPAIGN IDEAS

SOCIAL MEDIA CAMPAIGN

We need to stop interrupting what people are interested in & be what people are interested in.

CRAIG DAVIS

CAMPAIGN NAME

Give your campaign a memorable name that will make it easy for you to identify in the future.

CAMPAIGN OBJECTIVE

Brand awareness, reach, traffic, engagement, video views, messages, app installs, messages, catalog sales, store traffic.

DAILY / MONTHLY BUDGET

It takes the social media channel advertising algorithm a few days to identify who is most likely to take your desired call to action. Give yourself enough budget to start seeing results. Set your cost per click or cost per conversion goals.

START DATE - END DATE

CONVERSION EVENT (IE WEBSITE LINK)

SOCIAL MEDIA CAMPAIGN

Your ad copy wants to make your audience stop the thumb and take notice

JULIE HALL

AUDIENCE

After your creative, choosing the right audience is the most important part of any successful campaign. A mistake here can increase your ad spend significantly. It can sometimes take a while to find them, so do your research and make sure you complete the customer avatar sheets.

On Facebook and Instagram some of the things to consider are location, gender, age, interests, pages that they might like, stage of life. On LinkedIn consider size of company, job roles, individual organisations, business categories and LinkedIn groups.

SOCIAL MEDIA CAMPAIGN

Creativity without strategy is called art, creativity with strategy is called advertising

JEF RICHARDS

DISPLAY URL

The URL your audience sees on the ad.

DESTINATION URL

Where do you want to send them - you might want to think about creating a campaign specific URL using Google UTM Manager (link in the resource document).

WHERE YOUR AD IS GOING TO BE DISPLAYED

Each social channel has different options for this but consider whether you want to display your ads in stories, in the main feed, on videos and whether you want them to show up on mobile and/or desktop.

SOCIAL MEDIA CAMPAIGN

What you say in advertising is more important than how you say it

DAVID OGILVY

AD NAME

MEDIA

Single image, carousel, video, stories

PRIMARY TEXT

This is the first piece of copy that your audience will see and they will usually see it on preview. Make sure the first sentence is compelling so that your audience will click! It can be long or short depending on your copy strategy. Use the notes page at the end of this section if you are writing long copy.

SOCIAL MEDIA CAMPAIGN

Be creative while inventing ideas, but be disciplined while implementing them

AMIT KALANTRI

HEADLINE

This is often a statement that wil entice someone to click (keep it fairly short - at the time of print facebook has a limit of 40 characters).

DESCRIPTION

A statement that sits underneath the headline (at the time of print, facebook has a limit of 30 characters).

MEASURES

How many leads, clicks and conversions would you like to achive over what time period?

CAMPAIGN REVIEW

Great marketing makes your customer feel like you really understand them

JULIE HALL

RETURN ON INVESTMENT

how much you earned in comparison to how much you invested or spent on the campaign

RETURN ON AD SPEND

how much you earned from ads in comparison to how much you spent on them

CONVERSION RATE

how many people converted from your campaign (sales or leads)

COST PER LEAD / COST PER ACQUISITION

how much you spent on each lead or sale

WEBSITE VISITS

IMPRESSIONS

CLICK THROUGH RATE

COST PER CLICK

FUTURE IMPROVEMENTS

Marketing without *data* is like driving with your eyes *closed*

DAN ZARELLA

TRACKING RESULTS

FOLLOWER GROWTH

WK	DATE						
0							
1							
2							
3							
4							
5							
6							
7							
8							
9							
10							
11							
12							
13							

ENGAGEMENT TRACKER

DATE	POST	CHANNEL	LIKES	SHARES	COMMENTS	VIEWS/ REACH

ENGAGEMENT TRACKER

DATE	POST	CHANNEL	LIKES	SHARES	COMMENTS	VIEWS/ REACH

ENGAGEMENT TRACKER

DATE	POST	CHANNEL	LIKES	SHARES	COMMENTS	VIEWS/ REACH

ENGAGEMENT TRACKER

DATE	POST	CHANNEL	LIKES	SHARES	COMMENTS	VIEWS/ REACH

ENGAGEMENT TRACKER

DATE	POST	CHANNEL	LIKES	SHARES	COMMENTS	VIEWS/ REACH

NOTES

ADDITIONAL RESOURCES

Thanks again for purchasing this
Social Media Marketing Workbook & Planner!

Like this book?

If you have found it useful, it would be hugely appreciated if you could leave a review on Amazon.

Other books

Please feel free to share this workbook with your friends and colleagues. We also sell variations of this workbook with just the planning pages and campaign pages.

Additional resources

You can find links to all the Social Media Planner books and downloadable worksheets, additional marketing resources at

juliehallonline.com/smpresources

Happy Marketing!!

Julie

Printed in Great Britain
by Amazon

13700827R00108